D1122907

DISCOVERING
MARSEILLES

ISBN 2-86276-167-2

© Editions Jeanne Laffitte, 1988
All rights reserved in all countries
including the U.S.S.R. and Scandinavia

© Alfred Wolf, Christian Crès, Pierre Ciot,
Laurent Giraudou, Thierry Ibert, J.-M. Antoine,
photographs 1988, aerial views L. Sciarli

No part of this publication may be reproduced in any form or
by any means without permission from the publisher.
All rights of reproduction and representation of photographs
out of the context of this publication are reserved by the photographers.

DISCOVERING MARSEILLES

Text by
Jean BOISSIEU
english version by A.-B. REES

Photography by
Alfred Wolf, Christian Crès, Pierre Ciot,
Laurent Giraudou, Thierry Ibert, J.-M. Antoine.
Aerial views L. Sciarli

EDITIONS JEANNE LAFFITTE

Towards about 200 BC, a small group of hirsute fishermen set foot on an island in the Seine; there they constructed a few mud and reed huts. Marseilles had been a prosperous city for more than four centuries by that time. The erection of its strong ring of pink limestone walls was just being completed. With some 50,000 inhabitants, it was without doubt already one of the greatest cities in the West, equal to Rome, its senior by only a few decades. It was also the richest of ports, a trading empire whose ships, whilst perhaps not discovering America, at least found their way to Greenland and to Senegal. The rival of Carthage, and for a long time stubbornly opposed to the yoke of Rome, it was on its quays that the first Christian apostles were later to land — Paul perhaps amongst them — on this soil which was not yet that of France. However, the traces of this illustrious past are not all that obvious to the casual visitor, anymore than are those of its links with the Crusades or with the epoch when the harbour of Lacydon sheltered the most important naval port in the Mediterranean, and received kings and popes. On climbing the slopes of Notre Dame de la Garde, the cursory judgement of the Marquise de Sévigné springs all too readily to mind - 'On the whole, the atmosphere is quite wicked'. Marseilles, under a false veneer of talkative nonchalance, a city of action and of secrecy, never has been too concerned about its past. Caring little for looks, Marseilles has preferred to build warehouses rather than palaces. Too ready to poke fun at itself, just as much in prosperity as in hard times, Marseilles has always done itself less than justice.

Though not easy to get to know, nonetheless beautiful is this 2,500 year old city of some one million inhabitants today, with its 23,000 hectares — 57,000 acres — of land, ringed around by white rocks, and having 70 kilomètres of shoreline to it, a dozen villages and eight islands. Facing the ever-changing sea, on its coat-of-arms it bears a blue cross on a field of silver for it is as mystical as Lyon and more mercantile than Smyrna is....

Marseilles can invite you or reject you; but once you fall under her spell she will never let you go....

Situated at 43 degrees 30 latitude north and 3 degrees 06 longitude east, seven hundred years before the birth of Christ the future site of Marseilles was a semi-circular alluvial plain gently descending towards the sea from the foot of two rocky, pincer-like ranges, those of l'Etoile and of Marseilleveyre ; plain which was extended inland by the narrow, winding valley of the Huveaune, coastal river flowing down from the mountain of the Sainte Baume. To the north of the mouth of this stream, the limestone hill on which Notre Dame de la Garde now stands sheltered on its far side a roughly rectangular haven reached from the open sea only through a narrow channelway : what today is the Old Port.

Off to seawards, islands covered with thick vegetation formed a protective barrier for this harbour. On the Huveaune plain lived Celto-Ligurian tribesmen who grew sparse crops of cereals and raised cattle, sheep and goats. Even then this tribe bartered on the beach with the Greek sailors who had brought them civilisation.

The Birth of Massalia (600 BC).

The story goes that one day, 600 years before Christ, a crew of young Ionians exiled from Phocaea because of overpopulation there, landed on the beach of Lacydon harbour, bringing with them the effigy of their goddess, Artemis of Ephesus. They made a pact with the natives and sealed it with the marriage of the expedition's leader, Protis, to the daughter of the local chieftain. The Ionians founded a community on the rocky spur forming the northern bank of Lacydon. They called it Massalia and it prospered quickly, all the more so since they were soon joined by others from their home city when it fell into the hands of Cyrus's Persians in 540 BC.

Thus began the expansion of the Massaliots who set up trading posts in the interior — at **Mastramella,** now St. Blaise ; and at **Glanon,** near St. Remy-de-Provence — and above all on the coast : **Emporion** (Ampurias) in Catalonia ; **Agatha** (Agde) in Languedoc ; **Olbia** (Hyères) ; **Antipolis** (Antibes) ; and **Nike** (Nice). Massalia became powerful,

The coat of arms of Marseilles - 'an azure cross on a silver field

trading in tin from Britain and Spain and exchanging Greek wine and pottery for slaves throughout Gaul and to as far off as the Rhine and the Danube rivers. City able to finance the expeditions of Pythéas, the Navigator, who invented the notion of longitude and discovered Iceland, the Baltic, and the Vistula, whilst in Africa his emulators thrust as far south as Senegal.

A dangerous alliance (125 BC) and an unfortunate choice (50-49 BC)

But, in 125 BC, already allied with Rome, first against the Etruscans and then against the Phoenicians, Massalia called upon its redoubtable neighbour for help against the pressure of the Celto-Ligurians. The legions came, pacified the hinterland, and stayed. With the foundation of AQUAE SEXTIAE (Aix-en-Provence) an era of colonisation in depth began which left Massalia and its possessions like little pockets of indepen-

des Vestiges, Fort St. Jean, the cathedral and the Gate of Aix — la Porte d'Aix. As used to be the custom in olden days, the graves were put outside the town, over on the south bank, all along what would become Rue Sainte right up to a stone quarry cut at the foot of the rocky gully which descends the wooded slopes of La Garde. The first Christians buried their dead on this site. An underground gallery gave rise to a sanctuary where the relics of St. Victor, a martyr of the end of the 3rd. century AD, were venerated.

The church began to be organised. It is known that Marseilles had a bishop named Oresius from the Edict of Milan, 313 AD, in which Constantine guaranteed religious freedom. One of Oresius' successors, Proculus, began building a baptistry in the area of La Major, as well as several churches forming there a cathedral group (380 AD). Two Monasteries were established in 416 AD near the sanctuary of St. Victor. This was the start of a centre of religion the influence of which was to spread throughout Europe.

The Time of the Invaders
(5th to 10th centuries)

Precarious prosperity. With the decline of the western Empire, (the last Roman Emperor Remulus Augustula was dethroned by Odoacre in 476 AD) the great invasions commenced, starting in 405 AD. Between 406 and 410 successive waves of Franks, Vandals, Burgonds and Visigoths flooded in. In the fifth and sixth centuries Marseilles submitted to pillaging by Goths and Franks then recovered its prosperity as Arles declined. In the seventh and eighth centuries it allied itself with Arabs come from North Africa via Spain, considering them as its natural trading partners. As a consequence in 732, Charles Martel, following his victory at Poitiers, came at the head of his Franks to plunder and subjugate Marseilles. Abandoned by its new masters, Marseilles was again invaded several times by pirates, Saracens (838) and Greek Islanders (848). Life in the town was limited to the northern shore and there to the episcopal precincts of the Château Babon. In

dence. Only until the moment when Caesar confronted Pompey in civil war. The assembly of the timouchoi — the embodiment of the Massaliote oligarchy — backed the wrong horse, Pompey ! Caesar won and laid siege to the city which fell after six months. It was forced to accept a Roman garrison and lost all its possessions save Nice and the Isles of Hyères. Massalia had become Marseilles. Remaining Greek culturally, but weakened by the competition of Arles, while its physicians remained famed, the original port area, neglected, was gradually filled-in. A marsh formed in its place, where ropemakers grew cannabis (hence the future La Canebière).

The first Christians arrived in the footsteps of St. Paul.

Martyrs and Monks
(3rd to 5th centuries AD)

The town was confined to the shore north of the port — between what is today the Jardin

923 St. Victor was seized by the Saracens. The town almost disappeared from the map. At the end of the tenth century, in 983, the Marquis Guillaume (Guillaume the Liberator) and his brother Roubaud united the people of Provence and hurled the occupiers into the sea. The city took on a new lease of life.

Crusaders and Merchants (12th century)
Three towns in one

Marseilles revived and from then on became a threefold city. In the old town, the representative of the civil power — the Viscount — contested supremacy with the bishop, whilst the powerful monastery of St. Victor and its abbot governed the countryside all around where the vines and olives grew. But, starting in 1095 with the first crusade, merchants organised the maritime transport of soldiers, pilgrims and goods from Marseilles to the Levant and back. They set up trading posts in the Holy Land and bought from the impoverished Viscount their independence and their right to act together as a body. Under the distant and benevolent sovereignty of the Counts of Provence of the House of Barcelona Marseilles' behaviour became almost that of an independent republic.

The Angevin Dream
(13th - 15th centuries)

In 1252 the brother of Saint-Louis King of France, Charles d'Anjou, succeeded by marriage to the last count of the Catalan dynasty Raimond-Berenger V. During two hundred years the Angevin and his successors were to squander Provence's energies in the pursuit of a dream — the conquest of the Kingdom of Naples to which they pretended. Marseilles became their naval base. The merchant fleet armed for war. It was completely destroyed, however, off Palermo in 1282. The ensuing slump only came to an end with the establishment of the papacy at Avignon (1309-76). The abbot of St. Victor, Guillaume de Grimoard, became the sixth Pope at Avignon as Urban V. For a time his generosity halted a decline which was thereafter accelerated when the city was sacked in 1423 by Alphonse V of Aragon.

The last Count of Provence of the House of Anjou, the Roi René, erected the Tower of St. Jean to protect the entrance to the port. In keeping with his will, upon the death of his successor, Charles III, Marseilles and the rest of Provence passed into the hands of King Louis XI of France in December 1481. King Charles VIII in turn pursued the Napolitan dream. Marseilles and its oligarchy benefitted from this at first. In 1486 the town once more received the naval fleet and the arsenal for galleys was constructed. Louis XII enlarged it

Students in a natural setting at the Luminy campus.

during the Italian Wars (1494-1559). However the town was also twice besieged by Charles Quint in 1524 and in 1536. It was then that François I belatedly built the Château d'If to protect the town. He ensured the port's prosperity more effectively in 1535 when he entered into a treaty with the Great Turk. Following the example of the Venetians — their rivals in the Mediterranean — the Marseillais henceforth enjoyed freedom of transport and trade with the Orient.
It was the beginning of modern times for the town.

Pavane for a defunct independence
(16th - 17th centuries)

Marseilles wisely kept out of the Wars of Religion, yet, on the accession of Henri IV in 1589, couldn't resist backing the wrong cause — as once before between Pompey and Caesar — this time The catholic League. There followed seven years of independence but also of tumultuous dictatorship. Cazaulx, the leader, was assassinated by Libertat in 1596. Marseilles submitted to the king ; and

in 1599 he endowed Marseilles with France's first Chamber of Commerce. Richelieu strengthened the arsenal and added to the galley fleet. However, in its thirst for independence the town, with its typical lack of judgement, took sides with La Fronde against the young Louis XIV. More vindictive than his grandfather, Louis beseiged the town, determined to conquer it, and after entering by a breach in the battlements abolished its privileges and built the forts of St. Jean and of St. Nicolas — not to protect the town but to keep watch upon it ! (1660).

Constraints which had their advantages — Colbert lightened taxes, made Marseilles a free port and granted it exclusive trading rights with the Orient. From that time on these 'gentlemen of trade' shared the new Town Hall with the subjugated aldermen — and had their own ambassadors. The town spread along the quay de Rive Neuve on the south side of the harbour. The galleys were brought back from Toulon, the Arsenal shipyard grew in size. And although Pierre Puget's plan for the Place Royale fell through, it was nonetheless a period of intensive rebuilding which was to give Marseilles its baroque architectural character. In 1683 Lully granted Marseilles the rights for what would become the oldest opera theatre outside Paris.

From the Great Plague to the Empire
(1720 - 1814)

The economy revived. At the dawn of the 18th century Marseilles traded as much with the Levant as with the Americas. In 1720 the arrival of a ship carrying the plague — the **'Grand St. Antoine'** — provoked an epidemic which carried off 38,000 inhabitants out of a population of 75,000. This brought to a temporary halt an affluence which went on growing up until the wars of the Austrian Succession (1741 - 1746) and the Seven Years War (1756 - 1763), the effects of which were disastrous. Nevertheless, on the eve of the French Revolution, activity was at its height, resting on equipping and fitting out ships. The traders of Marseilles, importers of cereals, fats, wool, spices, cotton and eventually molasses, increased their profits by creating processing industries, becoming millers, soapmakers, sugar refiners, printers of cards and engravings, manufacturers of clothing and earthenware. Succeeding in getting rid of the galleys (which were sent to Toulon), and the naval dockyards in order to create a new district was a final demonstration of their power. (1748, 81, 87) When 1789 came they proved receptive to new ideas. It was the Marseillais who went to Paris in 1792 **with the battle song of the Rhine Army** - which became

'La Marseillaise'. But once again when Marseilles supported the Girondins because they favoured local autonomy, it was the Jacobin party which triumphed. Repression, terror, destruction followed. When Bonaparte made Marseilles the ·county seat in 1799 (18th Brumaire, 8th year of the Republic) there was hope for a short time. It didn't last. The Empire suppressed the port's fiscal privileges and the continental blockade spoiled business. By the return of the Bourbons in 1814, the town was ruined.

When Marseilles held the Keys to the Orient (1814 - 1914)

Throughout the length of the 19th century, and even before Napoleon III made up for his uncle's mistakes by giving the town its new cathedral, the Pharo and Longchamp Palaces, St. Charles Station and, best of all, the extension of the port to the northwards towards l'Estaque, Marseilles was to experience one of its greatest epochs. The arrival of the railway complemented the role of the shipping companies which were increasing in number, (Messageries Maritimes ; Compagnie de Navigation Mixte ; S.G.T.M. ; Paquet ; Fraissinet) and in operating range as sail gave way to steam and above all, from the moment when the opening of the Suez Canal in 1869 shortened the voyages to India, China and Japan. It was the Colonial Era. The traditional industries — soap, sugar and oleaginous products — modernised. The small workshops of old became huge factories. Red Marseilles tiles went off to cover Australian roofs ; the refining of sulphur and soda processing saw the beginnings of a chemical industry. The cosmopolitan character of the town became accentuated due to large-scale immigration from both the interior and the exterior. The 1914 - 1918 War only served to increase the vitality of a city proud to hold the Keys to the Orient....

Ebb-tide (1918 - 1945)

Between the two wars a continued apparent well-being hid a decadence of which the tragi-comic events of local party politics and the more or less fanciful exploitation of an image as 'city of crime' for a criminality not larger than that of Hamburg or Rotterdam, or any other major port were only the external symptoms. What actually was happening was that as some companies expanded, their capital escaped the control of those who had founded them and that power of decision became concentrated in Paris, initiating a trend which was transformed after 1950 into a gradual internationalisation of control. The Second World War and the German occupation cost Marseilles dearly in dead, in deportees and in material damages done. The entire historic district was blown up by dynamite in January 1943. In 1944 the port was mined and the entrance blocked by sunken vessels ; within a few months after its liberation all this had been repaired.

The port of Marseilles has always loved fantasies.

A Question Mark.

Since losing its autonomy in 1938, Marseilles had been under guardianship, like a colony. It returned to a normal status with the elections of 1953 which saw Gaston Deferre enter the Town Hall as Mayor. This Cévenol lawyer remained in office right up until his death in 1986. Under this long administration — his opponents called it a reign — he had not only the wounds of wartime to heal but also the backlog of fifty years of neglect to make up for, in a city the population of which was to grow from 500,000 to 1,000,000 (650,000 - 950,000 precisely) between 1955 and 1975 but where the facilities had remained unexpanded. This led to the construction of whole new districts to the north of the city, to internal motorways and the tunnelling of the Metro. (Thus the town centre can look like a building site at times — which can be rather

disconcerting !) Over the past forty years the municipal administration has been successful in this respect. It has met with less success in dealing with problems arising after the wars in Algeria and Indochina and the granting of independence to former colonies. Above all, and in part this is the fault of the remoteness of the decision-making centres, it has taken a long time, too long a time to understand the irreversible nature of the evolution — accelerated by the energy crisis — which ultimately is to doom entire sectors of dock and maritime activity as well as their capital equipment. Though postponed for a time by the demographic boom and the housing programme, since before 1980 the slump has hit ship repair, the food processing industry and even chemicals, despite 75 % of France's hydrocarbon traffic passing through the new port at Fos.

However there is no shortage of hopeful new activities for Marseilles in advanced technologies, whether in such as underwater research and maintenance (Offshore) where Comex leads the world, or in biological and medical research and computer sciences. The town's effort is now being concentrated upon education and training. The 50,000 students of the university colleges of Aix-Marseilles represent a fantastic pool of potential creativity — which is all the greater that the local researchers already work hand in glove with industry. (CNRS ; INSERM ; the Office of Geological and Mine Research ; research institutes in micro-electronics, robotics, and artificial intelligence). Recent measures are already beginning to bear fruit with the setting-up of the Chateau Gombert Technological Centre in the northern suburbs of the city. Though there will be problems and pitfalls, this is the direction Marseilles must take — whilst going on with the diversification of tertiary activities in developing a site the qualities of which are now beginning to be recognised — if it wishes to reduce unemployment, dispel the disquiet arising from ethnic-assimilation problems and finally fight its way back uphill towards full prosperity. Something which it has always managed to do, even through the darkest moments of its history.

THE ORIGINS OF MARSEILLES

If you come by car by the northern motorway your first view of Marseilles will take in quite an impressive panorama, with, right in the middle before you, a steep rock dominated by Notre Dame de la Garde and its tower topped by the gilded statue of the Virgin Mary. From the roundabout at Porte d'Aix, clear well-placed signs will direct you to the Centre Bourse, close to the Vieux Port, and its underground car park where you can leave your car. If arriving at Marseille-Provence Airport by 'plane or coming by train, you will end up at 'Gare Saint Charles' train station. From there the underground 'Metro' will convey you to its VIEUX PORT-HOTEL DE VILLE station.

You will emerge in sight of the *Quai des Belges* which runs along the head of the *Vieux Port* — old Lacydon harbour — and is at the foot of *La Canebière.* This will be the reference point for our itineraries. First let's get our bearings. Facing portwards, the north is off to our right. *Eglise St. Ferréol,* at one time the residence of the commander of the Templars, marks the beginning of *Rue de la République* by way of which one may reach *La Joliette.* The quay on the same side — the *Quai du Port* — is overlooked by the most ancient part of the town. The 17th century Mairie, the only building on the quay to have been spared destruction in World War II, shows its decorated façade amidst a row of postwar blocks. Up on the side of the hill are the pink-coloured arcades of the 18th century *Hotel Dieu* and the bell tower of les Accoules (14th century). A little further on, the 12th century Church of St. Laurent and the ancient beacon look down on the Tour du Roi René (King René's Tower) and on Fort St. Jean which, with the enormous fortress of St. Nicolas (17th century) across the harbour seem to bar the entrance to the port. There on the opposite southern side can be seen the Abbaye de St. Victor (5th, 13th, 14th centuries) with higher up in the background, Notre Dame de la Garde Basilica. The quay on that side is called the *Rive Neuve.* Approaching it, one can see the light-coloured façade of the one-time Criée aux Poissons, or fish market, now the National Theatre of Marseilles, and next, the buildings erected at the end of the 18th century on the site of the former galley arsenal.

This first sweeping glance covers in fact all the historical part of Marseilles which our walks will help us to explore. But, right now, there's nothing to stop us sauntering along, admiring the yachts, or getting to know the fishwives who sell freshly-landed fish each morning there where on Quai des Belges the white boats which ply to the islands tie up.

FIRST STROLL

Jardin des Vestiges - R. Reine Elisabeth - Pl. G. Péri - Qu. des Belges - Qu. du Port - Hôtel de ville - Pl. Jules-Vernes - Maison diamantée - Pl. Vivaux - Musée des Docks - Qu. du Port - Fort Saint-Jean - Av. St-Jean - R. H. Tasso - Pl. de Lenche - R. St-Laurent - Eglise Saint-Laurent - Espl. de la Tourette - Pl. de la Major - Cathédrales - Bd de la Major - R. A. Becker - R. de l'Evêché - R. J.-F. Leca - R. de l'Observance - FRAC - R. de la Charité - Vieille Charité - R. Rodillat - R. du Panier - Le Refuge - R. des Muettes - Pl. des Moulins - Montée des Accoules - Pl. Daviel - Hôtel-Dieu - Hôtel de Cabre - Grand'rue - R. de la République - Egl. Saint-Cannat-des-Prêcheurs

Rue de la République...

Les vestiges : Past and Present.

Hôtel-Dieu

*The Accoules clock overlooks
the port*

Church of S. Cannat des Prêcheurs

Hôtel de Cabre

This palace, long ago consecrated to Thémis...

You're not a 'Marseillais' if you've never eaten a 'chichi-fréji' (similar to a doughnut).

On emerging from the underground car park at the **Centre Bourse** back behind St Ferreol Church, we discover in the Jardin des Vestiges the Greek then Roman port which was at the origins of Marseilles. It doesn't need much imagination to see water lapping against the stones of the first century Roman quay instead of the green lawn and its cats at play, or to recognise the square cistern at one's feet where sailors came to take fresh water. Slightly to one side rise the thick, pink walls of limestone from La Couronne off on the Blue Coast. One can see the Hellenistic curtain-wall (300-200 BC) and three older towers, two of which frame the town's gate — entry of the East-West main-way which goes back to the sixth century BC and is still in name the 'high street'. This rampart was excavated almost by accident in 1967 during the reconstruction of the town centre; Julius Caesar kicked his heels before it during six

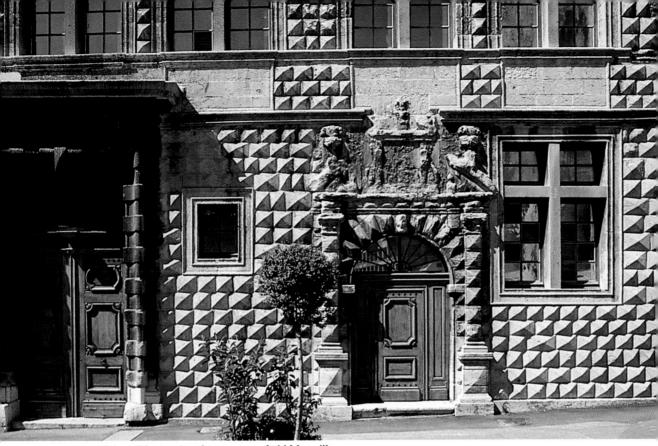

La Maison Diamentée - the museum of old Marseilles.

An 18th century miniature crèche in coral.

Old Tarot cards at the Musée du Vieux Marseille.

months : and now it is like a living extension to the **Musée d'Histoire** of which the most outstanding exhibit is undoubtedly the hull of a 3rd century merchant ship found embedded in mud on this site. Today this is preserved by the same process used to make instant coffee — lyophilisation : freeze-drying !

From the **Jardin des Vestiges** we join the **Quai du Port** passing by Eglise St. Ferréol, ancient commanderie of the Knights Templar. Only a few narrow-fronted old houses survived wartime destruction by the corner of the port there.

The remainder dates from the fifties; between Fernand Pouillon's sober frontages the **Hotel de Ville** is set like a jewel. Built between 1665 and 1674 to the plans of Guaspre Puget and Mathieu Portal on the site of the medieval Loge de Mer, there is a copy of the coat-of-arms sculpted by Pierre Puget on the façade. Initially the town aldermen met on the first floor whilst the officers of trade met on the ground floor. This gave rise to a curious characteristic: the building does not possess a staircase ; the first floor is reached by means of a bridge — covered in the 18th century — from an adjacent building ! Let us pass under this archway to Place Jules Vernes where the Maison Diamantée stands to one side of the square. This beautiful mansion owes its name to the diamond-shaped masonry of its front. Commenced in 1570 for the merchant Pierre Gardiolle and completed by an Italian architect, pupil of the Bolonais - Sebastino Serlio, for Nicola de Robbio, an inspector of artillery, between 1593 and 1620. It is now the headquarters of the **Musée du Vieux Marseille** in which are exhibited clothing, rare cradles and the oldest painting of the Port (15th century). One room is devoted to the ancient manufacture of playing cards (Tarot de Marseille) and another, with a wealth of detail, to the town centre during the riots of 1848. Next to Place Jules Vernes is Place de Vivaux where we will stop at the **Musée des Docks Romains.** Here an excellent display preserves part of the antique quay dating from the first century. This came to light during the reconstruction of this district. There are also clay objects and sculptures found during the archaeological digs. The

Le Panier - steps reaching up to the sky...

modern quay is quite near and we go back to it have a look at two buildings which once belonged to the quarantine service. *(Consigne sanitaire).* That on the right, on entering the courtyard, dates from 1716 ; the other is a faithful 19th century copy. Undergoing restoration nearby is the beautiful three-master *'Le Marseillois'.* Depending on the season, there are usually several old vessels tied up alongside it. Above us rises **Fort St. Jean** around which we go by way of the Promenade Louis Brauquier. Bygone Commanderie of the Knights of St. John of Jerusalem, rivals of the Knights Templar, (12th century), its keep was erected by Roi René in about 1423. The keep is 34 metres high (110 ft) and replaced the Tour Maubert destroyed when Alphonse of Aragon sacked the town. The Tour de Fanal, to the north, dates from 1644. The fort was gutted in August 1944, during the battle for the town's liberation. From the fort we now go to Place de Lenche, turning aside to see all that still remains of the Greek theatre of Marseilles. There are no more than a few stone steps in a square surrounded by school buildings. But Place de Lenche occupies the space and retains the rectangular shape of the ancient agora where the Assembly of the People sat. From its esplanade one can take in virtually all the panorama of the town and ports. The Church of St. Laurent — its restoration now being completed — was erected on the foundations of a Greek temple. It is in fact two parallel churches, one 12th century Romanesque and the other, St. Catherine's, dating from the start of the 17th century and having renaissance decoration and rib-vaulting. This archaic tendency to group sanctuaries together in oriental fashion was mirrored in the past by La Major, the old cathedral to which the esplanade of La Tourette leads us. This originally consisted of several juxtaposed churches and a baptistry. All that now remains are an 11th century apse, one of the five bays of the nave and its 12th century aisles. Inside, there is a 15th century ceramic relief, 'The Descent from the Cross', attributed to one of the Della Robbia, and a sculptured marble reredos of St. Lazare of about 1480 by Francesco

La Chapelle de la Charité - Pierre Puget's masterpiece.

Laurana. The remainder was razed to the ground from 1852 in order to build the present gigantic neo-byzantine cathedral. Underneath it is hidden the octagonal baptistry of circa 380 AD built during the episcopacy of Proculus (excavations are under way). Even if there is a tendancy to see the style of the Second Empire, which left Marseilles with some undeniable successes, in a more favourable light today, one can only regret such a loss. One may console oneself by visiting the FRAC collection of paintings and sculpture in the former Convent of l'Observance and above all by the sight of the **Vieille Charité.** Here, three floors of pink stone galleries harmoniously enclose a baroque chapel. This has an elliptical-plan dome and was started about 1679 by Pierre Puget and completed after his death by his son, François in 1694. This ensemble, radiant with light, was restored between 1970 and 1986 and today constitutes a centre for several bodies for a variety of cultural activities — in particular musical ones. A number of exhibition rooms have been equipped to accommodate temporary shows in the plastic arts ; of these the Salle Allende, is devoted to photographic displays. Finally, since 1988 have been on show there the Egyptian (Clot Bey Fund) Etruscan, Celto-Ligurian (portico and statuary from the Roque-pertuse sanctuary) ancient Oriental (Suse,

At the Vieille Charité.

The Celto-Ligurian bi-frontal Hermes at the Musée Archéologique.

Egyptian sarcophagus : Porte d'Orient, Marseilles.

Khorsabad, Chypre) pre-Hellenic, Greek and Roman collections — the latter with the exception of exhibits of local origin, now in the Musée d'Archeologie Méditerranéen (see hereafter). But that doesn't alter the fact that the Charité was originally an institution having more of the prison than the poorhouse about it ! Unfortunates caught by the 'beggar hunters' (chasse-gueux) and abandoned children were secluded here. The latter at least were given training which would enable them to find work in the shipyard workshops or on board ship. One finds this inclination towards imprisonment — typical of Louis XIV's reign — again nearby at the Convent du Refuge. This was a prison for loose women *(les femmes de mauvaise vie).* It is nowadays a gallery for temporary exhibitions.

There remain only two, albeit arm-less, windmills out of all those which once turned merrily on the **Place des Moulins,** but the spot is still charming and delightfully rustic in character today. This is the heart of the district known as **Le Panier** -The Basket- after one of its streets. All these narrow lanes and alleyways, remaining just as they were in the Middle Ages, bear picturesque names — Les Belles Ecuelles 'The Lovely Bowls' ; Le Poirier 'The Peartree' ; Les Repenties 'The Penitents' ; Les Muettes 'The Dumb Women'. Going by way of the **Montée des Accoules** we pass by a tower — all that's left of a church destroyed during the reign of Terror — and arrive in front of the beautiful **Hôtel Dieu,** built on the foundations of a 12th century hospital by Mansart-le-Jeune in 1753-82. From there, in the **Grand Rue** we pass by the former Palais de Justice (18th century) erected by the Gérard brothers, with sculptures by Verdiguier, and the mansion built for the magistrate, **Louis de Cabre,** in 1535. In 1954, this was moved — in one piece — on a gigantic truck, turned and brought into alignment with the new streets. Arriving at Rue de la République we cross over to look at the church **Saint Cannat des Prêcheurs,** before going back to our starting point. Begun in 1526 for the Dominicans and completed in 1739 by the Gérard brothers, the façade and interior decoration are baroque in style. The great organ was constructed in 1742 by Brother Isnard to whom we are also indebted for that of St. Maximin and of La Madeleine, in Aix-en-Provence. As to the Rue de la République itself, it was built during the Second Empire by Bodin. With its sculptured frontages it is a good example of Hausmannian townplanning.

The old cathedral :
remarkable Romanesque architecture.

The Cathedral of Notre Dame La Major and the old cathedral.

Place des Moulins : a provincial change of scenery.

St. Laurent's Church paired with St. Catherine's Church.

The Place de Lenche, possible site of a Greek Agora.

L'Hôtel de Ville (town hall) - the house without stairs !

At the Musée des Docks Romains.

GALLEY SLAVES ; MONKS AND LEGIONNAIRES

In humbling Marseilles, Louis XIV did the town a proud service. Thanks to him, the tight belt of ancient bulwarks was shattered. Within a few years Marseilles' area was quadrupled. If the aldermen of the time had followed the dream of their illustrious compatriot, Pierre Puget, the sculptor, townplanner and architect, today we would be able to see on the site of La Canebière a veritable pleasure garden, ovalshaped, surrounded by wide canals with a Triumphal Arch opening on to the port front. Rather than dream, the Aldermen counted their silver crowns. Nevertheless, apart from the forts which stand guard at the mouth of the port, Louis XIV, the Sun King, left his mark on the map of Marseilles. The lines of the streets from Fort St. Nicolas right up to the church of Notre Dame du Mont, and from there up to St. Charles Station exactly cover the bulwarks of the 17th century fortifications. From our chosen observation point at the end of the Vieux Port, the right-hand side — the Quai du Port — corresponded to the Greco-Roman and

The Vieux-Port entrance from the Pharo gardens.

above all to the Middle Ages. With the one exception of the Abbey of St. Victor, to the left-hand side — the Quai de Rive Neuve — are attached all the images of absolute monarchy, of the time of the galleys and of their galley slaves. Still, it must be borne in mind that it was Charles VIII who established the galley shipyards in 1486, and that, at the height of its development, this extended not only over the quadrilateral bounded by Cours Jean Ballard and Cours d'Estienne d'Orves, but also from Quai des Belges to Rue Paradis. This ancient topography is corroborated by the names of Rue Pavillon (Flag St) and Rue de la Darse (Harbour St).

Hôtel de Ville : Louis XIV — the Sun King.

Fishermen mending their nets on the port.

St. Ferréol church.

SECOND STROLL

***Parc automobile des Arsenaux - Capitaine-
rie des galères - r. Fort-Notre-Dame - r.
Neuve-Sainte-Catherine - Pl. St-Victor - La
basilique abbatiale de Saint-Victor - r.
Sainte - Rampe St-Maurice - Fort Saint-Ni-
colas - av. Charles-Livon - Jardin et palais
du Pharo - Qu. de Rive Neuve - Le Caréna-
ge - l'Amadeus - La Criée - Port de Plaisance - le ferry-boat.***

From the Vieux Port metro entrance or the
N⁰ 83 bus stop, the ***Quai des Belges,*** with its
daylong, colourful bustle and its morning
glitter of fishstalls, stretches southwards by
way of the ***Cours Jean Ballard,*** at right angles
to the ***Quai Rive Neuve.*** The four massive
blocks with deep cornices fronting this have
their exact counterparts on the other side of

Commemorative plaque to Alexander Ist.

28

Cafe terraces on the quay des Belges.

La Canebière in the sunshine.

Seafood...

and trimmings !

Vieux Port's tranquil mirror.

The fishermen return.

street running on parallel to the quay to form Place Thiars complete with its fountain. Nowadays this quadrilateral is known as the *îlot Thiars,* a reminder of the time, prior to 1926, when it was enclosed by a canal now filled in. This went round two right angled bends, occupying the central portions of Cours d'Estienne d'Orves en route, as well as of Place Aux Huiles, there to rejoin the port. It was the site of part of the galley slaves' hospital and of the dry docks where galleys were built and repaired. The navy ceded the yard to the town in the 18th century, and this ensemble began to be built in 1781. Intended for use as warehouses for the shipping trade, it was erected by a pupil of Nicolas Ledoux — at that time constructing the Palais de Justice in Aix-en-Provence. The interior courtyards, the staircases with their wrought ironwork grills, and the extensive premises are left as witnesses of the brief period of this use. Following the slump of the Revolution and of the Empire periods, the port's activities were transferred to La Joliette where new, bigger docks were being made. The yard then became the home for crafts activities whilst the canal, originally used for internal circulation in the shipyard, became the haven for fishing boats. Later the district became that of the newspaper printers and of artists. Jean Ballard founded the literary revue *« Les Cahiers du Sud »* at Nº 10 in 1924 publishing the greatest writers — from Paul Valéry and Saint-John Perse to Miguel Angel Asturias and Sengor — up until 1966.

After a variety of misadventures *Cours d'Estienne d'Orves* itself, for long encumbered by the huge bulk of a concrete car park, has just been remodelled. The parking lots are buried in the depths of the bygone canal. Over them stretches a pedestrian mall which was designed like a scaled-down reminder of Pierre Puget's projected Place Royale; this has layout and street furniture by Charles Bové.

The most interesting side from the point of view of links with the past and for present day activities is that bearing odd numbers. The builders of the later 18th century, being thrifty, incorporated a lot of the earlier edifices into their own constructions. The

Capitainerie de l'Arsenal - Cours d'Estienne d'Orves.

Place Thiars in the Arsenal district.

rotunda at the corner of the Rue Breteuil has kept the form of the tower that once stood at this spot. Next to the building of 'La Marseillaise' — last survivor of the former newspaper district — the present-day headquarters of the Mutuelle de Marseille is in a mansion (entered by n⁰ 42 Rue Sainte) which retains all its pompeyan interior decoration intact. The only piece of evidence of the 17th century arsenal still to be intact today is the façade of N⁰ 21 (Hôtel Urbis). Shown on old plans as the Grand Escalier du Bagne it is known nowadays as the **Maison du Capitaine.**

However, behind this façade, as with all the others, one can follow the internal alignment of the arches of the onetime ropeworks — a double-row of buildings drawn up over a distance of 250 metres (812ft). These traces are particularly easy to see at N⁰ 25, **Les Arcenaulx** — a lively complex, headquarters of publishers Jeanne Laffitte, with a book-shop, restaurant and tearoom on the premises as well as conference and exhibition rooms, antique shop, and above, on the upper floors, reached by an interesting staircase, an art gallery and art and craft studios. On the square itself and the neighbouring Carré Thiars, the good-natured traditions of the epoch when this district was that of newspapers, markets and boatbuilders is maintained by the cafés and seafood restaurants.

But very few people would be able to tell you of the existence of another, almost complete, relic of the king's former shipyard, the semi-circular blinded arches and the first floor of the buildings on the odd-numbered side of **Place aux Huiles.** Storeys have been added to them since the time when they were the provision and fittings stores where galleys were got ready before sailing.

This square was for many years the annual setting for two traditional fairs; that of garlic, sold in long strings, and the Taraiettes Fair, selling miniature pottery teasets, and other chinaware for children. We join Rue Fort Notre Dame by climbing the steps at the far upper corner of the square. From there it doesn't matter whether we go up the hill and turn right on Rue Sainte or go down and take

Rue Neuve-Ste-Catherine. Here, in the cellars of the buildings, are the foundations of the soap works of which the acrid fumes must have really made the air foul in former days. Deeper buried still lies an ancient cemetery attributed at one time with the same sacred character as that of the Alyscamps at Arles. Whence the street names: Rue Paradis and Rue Sainte. Whichever street was taken, both meet in front of the Basilica of St. Victor. From here, high up, one can look down on the sparkling surface of the old careening basin where ships' hulls were formerly scraped and recaulked. Nowadays it is ringed around by the road connecting up with the tunnel under the Vieux Port. The bulk of the upper fort, St. Nicolas, just beyond this, is somewhat overwhelming whilst the lower fort links up with the shore, hiding from view the Pharo Gardens. Frieze-like, across the port, are to be seen Fort St. Jean, La Tourette, the town hall, the roofs of the Old Town all jammed up together and among which the dome of La Charité can just be made out, and beyond in the distance against the blue of the sky, the rocky crags of the Etoile range. Behind us stand the 18th century houses built by the canons who took over from the monks when Louis XV secularised the abbey in 1774. Saint Victor, mother church of the Benedictine community which bore this name, has a castlelike look to it — an appearance which must have been even more striking before the dismantlement carried out during the Terror by the Jacobins, reputedly, but already been prepared for execution in the latter years of the Old Regime. The irreparable harm done dates in fact from after the Concordat of 1801. Previously the monastic buildings starting from the apse of the abbeychurch included both Rue de l'Abbaye and the Rue Commandant Lamy which runs at right angles to it. Southwards they covered a segment of the Avenue de la Corse delimited by Rue d'Endoume and Rue du Rempart, so far as Rue Sauveur Tobelem. The Gardens covered the whole area between Rue Commandant Lamy and the foot of the fort.

From the Rue de l'Abbaye can be seen, on the north face of the church, the original level

Traditional delicacies - from the gâteau des Rois to the navettes de la chandeleur.

34

Night-time ; Notre Dame de la Garde watches over Saint Victor.

The nave of the Abbatial Basilica of St. Victor.

The former fishmarket — Criée aux Poissons — the National Theatre of Marseilles has kept the name.

of the monks cloisters as well as two arched doorways.

The left-hand doorway is decorated on the under-curve of the arch — the 'archivolt' — by a moulding and five carved bands of palm-fronds. (11th century Romanesque). Before being walled up this doorway led into a passage over an arch bestriding the atrium, or courtyard of the original sanctuary, which we will look at later. For the moment, after a glance at the extremely severe-looking main gable, we will go round the church to on the south side, passing at the foot of the apse which is topped by defensive battlements or 'merlons'. On the north side, the two square towers — said to be of Urbain V and of Izarn — are actually defensive bastions. The first tower, that containing the bells, is nearest to the chancel and adjoins the veritable little open-to-the-sky fortress built on this. This tower is similar in construction to those on the ramparts at Avignon. One enters the upper church by a porch in the d'Izarn tower. The nave has four barrel-vaulted bays whilst the aisles, the transept and the chancel have intersecting ribs. All this is the fruit of a 13th century restoration carried out by the sacristan Hugues de Glazinis; the chancel, however, was completed during the 14th century on the orders of Pope Urban V, formerly Guillaume de Grimoard, Abbot of St. Victor and pope at Avignon from 1361. The sepulchral monument erected to his memory can be seen in the chancel. Walking

A forest of masts on the Vieux-Port.

The traditional garlic fair - La Foire à l'aïl.

37

The careenage basin at the port entrance with St. Jean Fort, Roi René tower and church of St. Laurent in the background.

The ferry-boat ; no need to mention Marcel Pagnol !

around the upper church interior, we pause to look at the fine painting of the Virgin, pregnant and kneeling, by Michel Serre (1658-1733). Up in the chancel vault, the keystone is a medallion representing St. Victor on horseback, brandishing a sword (circa 1365). There is a palaeo christian tomb, recently excavated, of the fifth century on the right-hand side of the aisle. In very good condition, it held the body of a woman clad in gold-embroidered white cloth. On her brow there was a small gold cross. The sarcophagos represents, from left to right, the Sacrifice of Abraham, Christ between St. Paul and St. Peter, and the Healing of the Blindman. In the chapel of the Holy Sacrament, to the left at the rear of the church, the fifth century tabular, palaeo christian altar is decorated with two carved friezes, the first of a ewe and the other of doves. The crypt, or more exactly the lower church, is reached by a door below the organ. It is rather difficult to give a detailed description of what is, perhaps, the oldest Christian sanctuary in France, because it is arranged around a martyry cut out of the rock, and which contains under the altar the double tomb of two unknown martyrs of the persecution of Dèce (249-251). This is the original church, preceded by an atrium unfortunately robbed of its marble columns in Napoleonic times. Under the entrance arch there is a fifth century stucco decoration; under another, the traces of a mosaic of the same period. At the same level there are some caves or grottos — primitive catacombs. In the first of these, called St. Lazare, there is a carving in low relief of the Magdalen, from Puget's workshop. The martyry is continued by a narrow nave ending at the Chapel of St. Andrew. This corresponds to the porch of the upper church (under the Izarn tower). Recent excavations, to the right of the altar in the chapel, have unearthed a mass of tombs. A wider nave, parallel to the first and completed by a square room, as it appears at present, corresponds to 13th century work. Of which above the pillar, a fresco. Under the entrance steps one can see Izarn's tombstone in a funerary niche. The recumbent figure and

inscription date from the 11th century. (circa 1047) This Catalonian monk reformed the abbey which was originally founded in about 416 by the oriental anchorite, Cassien. This sanctuary, dedicated to Notre Dame de Confession, radiates spirituality but is, nonetheless, at the same time an extraordinary lapidary museum. It would take hours to examine the Roman and palaeochristian tombs, sculptures and inscriptions — including the controversial 3rd century ones of Volusianus and Fortunatus. Martyrs perhaps — but more probably sailors lost at sea.... Better to allow oneself be captivated by the spell of the place — revived each year at Candlemas by the strange ceremony of the Green Candles.

Afterwards on leaving one might go along to

Look — these are 'Taraïettes' !

the nearby baker's and buy there a few 'navettes' - the little, hard biscuits made to a secret recipe related to the same tradition. For until 1781 this was the monastery's bakery !

Next we will go to **Boulevard Charles Livon** - extension of Quai Rive Neuve - by way of St. Maurice' Ramp and its tunnel. In its gardens, which swarm with children, stands the Palais du Pharo. This palace was Napoleon III's present to Empress Eugénie in 1856. Palace which she gave ungrudgingly to the town after 1871. From the green lawns there is a panor-

Memories of Empress Eugénie hover around the Palais du Pharo...

ama which takes in the sea, the ports and the town. The view of the Old Port is exactly the same as that chosen by Joseph Vernet for a painting now in the Musée de la Marine in Paris. Returning towards the centre we stroll past the sailing boats at the quayside. *'The Amadeus'* — twin of the *'Marseillois'* moored near the Tour du Roi René and which we saw earlier — is a big fishing cutter which only puts to sea to sail in the roadstead on musical mini-cruises — which is how it got its name !

The onetime *'Criée aux Poissons'* farther along used to be where catches of fish were auctioned off but now houses the Théâtre National de Marseille behind its turn-of-the-century glassed façade. Its director is Marcel Maréchal. Inside are to be found two theatres ; the 800-seater Louis Guilloux Hall and the 250 seat Jacques Audiberti Hall. Planned out by the stage designer Guillemot they form part of one of the most complete theatrical complexes in France. The theatre opened in 1981.

The panorama of the port and the old town from the battlements of Fort St. Nicolas.

Still following the quay we must cast a sentimental look aside for the quaint craft — almost a floating tramcar — which shuttles to and fro across the old port. This is the **Ferry Boat** so dear to the heart of Marcel Pagnol. Close by is the yachting club — the **'Société Nautique'.** At all times of the year its clubhouse — looking like the restaurant of a cruise liner from the past — is the rendezvous of everyone who matters in the yachting world, both in the 'Med.' and elsewhere. Whenever there is a big international sailing competition the club's floating pontoon is all decked out with bunting.

The 17th and 18th century buildings here are called 'domaines' (note at Nº 18 the restaurant 'Chez Maurice Brun' — the 'academy' of Provençal gastronomy). With little interior alleyways, they were built on the site of the ancient residence 'Les Jardins du Roi'; mansion of the Counts of the House of Anjou, Kings of Naples, and Governors of Provence when they came to Marseilles.

IN THE STEPS OF THE MARQUIS DE SADE.

Our third circuit of discovery again starts from the port and takes us over the visible traces of Marseilles' development from the time of Louis XIV. Prior to Louis the naval dockyards of the arsenal almost completely blocked access to the present-day Quai des Belges but beyond Rue Paradis there were only a few houses in the fields and some convents amongst the vineyards, orchards and vegetable patches.

THIRD STROLL

La canebière - Pl. Gl de Gaulle - R. Pythéas - R. Beauvau - L'Opéra - R. Francis-Davso - R. Grignan - Musée Cantini - R. Grignan - R. Estelle - R. d'Aubagne - Pl. N-D. du Mont - R. Fontanges - R. St-Michel - Pl. J.-Jaurès (La Plaine) - R. des 3 Mages - Pl. Carli - Conservatoire et Archives - Cours Julien - Les Bernardines - Marché des Capucins - R. Rodolphe-Pollack - R. Rouvière - R. de la Palud - R. de Rome - Maison de Pierre Puget - Crs St-Louis - Canebière

*La Canebière
finishes at the end of the earth...*

Marseilles pretty métro isn't a toy !

La Canebière is no more than an avenue a kilometre long. However the words of the song say it **reaches to the ends of the earth ;** it all depends on how you look at it !

It ends, in fact, at the flagstones which separate the quay from the water. Let's follow it for a few steps along. Facing the Palais de la Bourse (we can go to see the Musée de la Marine and its model ships another time) is a square — the Place Général de Gaulle. Just here King Alexander of Yugoslavia and a French minister, Louis Barthou, were shot dead by a Croatian terrorist on the 9th of October 1934. It was on this square that the imposing edifices of the arsenal were spread out, around the Pavillon de l'Horloge which left its name to **Rue Pavillon.** Going by way of Rue Pythéas and Rue Beauvau — of which the poet-adventurer Louis Brauquier sang — we arrive before the **Opera.** This is not the one authorised to open by Lully in 1683 — the oldest in the provinces — nor even the opera built between 1780 and 1787. The fire which destroyed that one in 1919 only left the Ionic colonnade by Benard, behind which the architects Castel, Ebrard and Raymond erected a silver and marble nave, embellished with sculptures by Bourdelle and de Sartorio. Constructed between 1921 and 1924, it is a fine example of the Art-Deco style. Passing round the opera we cross Rue Francis Davso and enter Rue Grignan. Nos 62 and 60 on the even-numbered side of the street are decorated with beautiful wrought iron work of the Louis XVI period. Opposite, at N⁰ 53, is the Hôtel de Paul, a residence dating from 1760. On the corner of Rue Paradis, which we cross, we find Hôtel Pascal built in the year of Louis XV's death in 1774. A few steps further along, at N⁰ 19, the Compagnie du Cap Nègre, which held the coral monopoly on the Algerian coast, had a magnificent mansion erected, in 1694. Its last owner, the patron Jules Cantini, presented it to the town in 1916. It is now the **Cantini Museum.** His famous collections of over six hundred items of 17th and 18th century earthenware from Marseilles, St. Jean du Désert and Moustiers are now displayed in the panelled halls of Château Borély — a museum of decorative arts and furnishings. Enlarged in 1986 by the

addition of an adjoining hall offering airy accommodation for temporary exhibitions, the mansion encircles a charming garden-patio. Its role as museum of Modern Art, created in 1951 by the enthusiasm of Jacques and Marielle Latour, is now being reinforced. Works by Paul Signac, Raoul Dufy, Albert Marquet, (Le Port de Marseille) once at the Palais Longchamp, have joined an important

L'Opera born in 1787 - and still going strong !

surrealist collection including Picabia, Jacques Hérold, André Masson, Giorgio de Chirico, Roberto Matta. This recalls the fact that Marseilles was the haven of Surrealism in 1940 before the exile of André Breton.

The collection is no less rich in representatives of more recent movements : figurative with Adami, Alechinsky, Francis Bacon, Balthus, Bret, Crémonini, Music, Pignon, Prassinos, Segal ; non-figurative in its various trends : Debré, Estève, Sam Francis, Hartung, Manessier, Riopelle, Soulages, Tapièes, Vieira da Silva. These form quite a good panorama of the 40's and 60's. However, in this living museum, in which the collections are continually growing, all the trends and contemporary experiments: figurative narration, new realism, surface/

45

'Port of Marseilles' by Albert Marquet circa 1916.

'Monument to the Birds' by Max Ernst. 1927.

support, minimal *(arte povera),* informals — without forgetting the photographic section — are judiciously represented around the metal sculptures of the locally born artist, Cesar — with a justifiable tendency to favour movements of Mediterranean origin.

The wealth of, and the continual addition to the reserves, means that exhibitions change quickly. On the top floor, however, the study centre and library are open to specialists.

The personnel — from attendants up — are pleasant and helpful. This is characteristic of all the Marseilles museums and is well worth mentioning. Highly accessible, the museums accommodate concerts (of contemporary and experimental music especially) and conferences. A very active association promotes links between the museum curators and the general public.

Rue Estelle — named after one of the town councillors at the time of the Plague of 1720 — is the prolongation of Rue Grignan. It joins Rue d'Aubagne, once the Grand

The Musée Cantini - contemporary art in a 17th century private residence.

Rue Saint-Ferréol.

The Provençal 'santons' have a rendezvous each year at the Allées Meilhan.

Two images of the Cours Julien - once a market place, now an 'in' place !

Place Carli : secondhand booksellers in front of the Conservatoire.

La gare de l'Est ; the last tram terminus…

La Chapelle des Bernardines - after the Revolution it became a museum - nowadays it is a try-out theatre.

...is also a transport museum !.

Chemin d'Aubagne, which spans Cours Lieutaud by a narrow bridge. At **Place Notre Dame du Mont** the church — rebuilt during the Restoration — has a very fine organ at the end of the nave. The altar from the original shrine is to be seen in the Chapel of the Sacré Coeur. We follow the façade of this church and arrive at Place Jean Jaurès, which the Marseillais call 'La Plaine'. This raised plateau is the daily scene of a bustling market. On a frontage at the corner of Rue de la Bibliothèque there is a rather ugly bas-relief commemorating the first aerial link by aerostat between Marseilles and Corsica. From **La Plaine** we go down to Place Carli by way of the Rue des Trois Mages — the three wisemen — named after a bygone inn. Here we find the building in pink and white stone erected by Esperandieu (1864 to 1869) which nowadays houses the Conservatory of Music, the National Ballet of Marseille and the Town

Archives — very welcoming and rich in rare manuscripts as well as having a particularly interesting collection of medals. From the bookstalls outside, we join Cours Julien, once a market square but now recently been substantially remodelled into an urban garden with fountains and greenery. It has become a pleasant centre of activity with galleries, boutiques and tempting restaurants all around. Retracing our footsteps, we pass before the baroque chapel of the **Bernardines** (1751) today an experimental theatre. Its neighbouring convent became Lycée Thiers in

The Boulevard Chave and its tramcars.

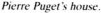

Pierre Puget's house.

1805 : amongst this highly reputed secondary school's illustrious former pupils — apart from Thiers himself of course — were Marcel Pagnol and the author of *'Belle du Seigneur'*, Albert Cohen. Let's now cross over Cours Lieutaud (sometimes easier said than done so heavy is the traffic !). Immediately on our right a little street leads us down to the **Market of Capucins** where there is the terminus for the last tramway in Marseilles. Though it does run for part of its route underground, don't confuse it with the Metro. The terminus building itself now serves as an amusing miniature museum of public transport. By way of Rue Rodolphe Pollack, or Rue Longue des Capucins — a busy, narrow street as spicy-smelling as an oriental market — we arrive at the end of Rue d'Aubagne. Here we must not miss N⁰ 15B ! This house — so dear to the Surrealists — was the theatre of the love-making done on the 27th of June 1772 which sent the famous Marquis de Sade to the Bastille !

Then by Rue Rouvière to the junction of Rue de la Palud and Rue de Rome. The house on the corner was built in 1681 by the sculptor and architect Pierre Puget for his own use. On the column in front of the house is a bust of the sculptor. At this time he had just finished the 'Milon de Croton' and had begun to work on his never-to-be-achieved Place Royale project. But in 1690 he began to build himself what his fellow townsmen considered a little palace. This was somewhat farther away, at that time out in the country, encircled by vineyards and gardens, but now the Rue Dieudé and Rue Fongate. Of this residence nothing seems to remain ; Puget died there on December 2nd, 1694.

On returning towards La Canebière, Rue de Rome widens to become Cours Saint Louis (on the other side of the Canebière the prolongation is called Le Cours Belsunce). Because of the shops with their particularly hideous fronts and signs, it takes a real effort of the imagination to realise that we are in fact facing a group of buildings of exceptional quality dating back to the late 17th and early 18th centuries.

Oyster sellers on the Cours St Louis…

…and florists.

IMPERIAL CASCADES

From now on our excursions will be mainly concerned with the Marseilles of the Second Empire. Distances will be greater and the centres of interest further apart. We can choose a public holiday and go by car or take public transport. The Métro is practical and pleasant with its individually styled stations, murals and bas-reliefs — but it is 'blind'. Better catch a bus ! Booklets of tickets and the **up-to-date** route guide and timetable are available at the R.T.M. kiosk on Cours Jean Ballard.

The Plage Estrangin fountain.

The Palais de Justice.

The Préfecture.

Since it is the overall impression which is important we won't enter into details on this rather long circuit. At Cours Pierre Puget (bus) the statue of the artist is a poor work by Lombard (1905). Place Estrangin is unworthy of its proportions and the fountain by Allard (1890). Rue d'Armeny bears the name of an Armenian merchant ennobled during the 17th century. Fine 18th century mansions, above all at N⁰ 11 — now an officers mess but once the residence of the Commanding General of the Army. The Préfecture building, by Martin, was begun in 1861 and knew its hours of bloodshed at the time of the Commune in 1871. Cours Lieutaud can be reached on foot unless one prefers to continue by bus down Rue St Ferréol, round into La Canebière and up past the neo-gothic church des Réformés, which stands on the site of a monastery of barefoot Carmelites (called Reformed Augustinians).

The upper part of La Canebière - once known as Les Allées de Meilhan - is the site of the traditional annual Foire aux Santons, fair at which Christmas crib figurines clad in Provençal costume are sold. Opposite in La Rue du Théâtre Français is the charming **Salle du Gymnase** now restored to the original state in which it opened in 1801.

Palais Longchamp was the gracious gift of Napoléon III to the town he loved — but which did not return his affections. Its cascades are in fact the overflow from the first water tower which supplied the town. The wing to the right of the columns houses the museum — mainly notable for its aquariums. The Musée des Beaux-Arts is in the left hand wing. The staircase murals are by Puvis de Chavannes. The museum — recently remodelled by the architect François Guy — has collections extending from the primitives to the impressionists. Among its strong points are works by Carrache, Rubens, Philippe de Champaigne and also Corot, Courbet, and Monticelli. There is an exceptional Bonnard of 1893 **'La Femme aux bas noirs'**. In its exhibition halls — one dedicated to Puget, and the other (complete with his sculptures) to Daumier — the museum also places emphasis on the 19th century Orientalist painters and above all on the forgotten artists

A typical building on the Canebière.

At the Palais Longchamp.

Marseilles from the church of Les Réformés.

The Palais Longchamp and its cascade.

'Christ and the woman taken in adultery' by Tiepolo. Musée des Beaux Arts.

'Gateway to the Orient' by Puvis de Chavannes. Palais Longchamp.

The gardens at Longchamp.

The Natural History museum.

Musée Grobet-Labadie.

Table setting at the Grobet-Labadie museum.

of Provence who worked in the spirit of Caravaggio during the 17th century : Finsonius, Faber, Reynaux-Levieux and Michel Serre. A special setting shows off the collection of African Art donated by the collector, Pierre Guerre.

Beyond the gardens we pass close at hand by the **Astronomic Observatory** founded by Leverrier in 1863. Our destination is the church **des Chartreux,** the neo-classical architecture of which may have followed a plan by Puget (1680). The square in front of the church retains the proportions of the entrance to the monastery established there in 1633. This was a dependancy of La Chartreuse de Villeneuve-lez-Avignon. The cells have been absorbed into later constructions.

On the homeward path we pause before the **Musée Grobet-Labadié** — almost facing Palais Longchamp — which preserves intact the home environment of a music-loving collector of the end of the 19th century. Exhibits include ceramics, miniatures and furniture. Outside on the wall is a monumental 'trompel'oeil' representing the donors, Louis Grobet and his daughter, Marie Labadié. This dates from 1985 and is by Campana.

L'église de l'ancienne Chartreuse.

The steps at the St. Charles station.

PATHWAYS TO THE SEA

A circuit for leisure lovers: the sun, the sea, the hills, harmonious homes and picturesque palaces. On this excursion the best thing to do is to copy the Marseillais; every Sunday afternoon they drive slowly along, bumper to bumper, so as not to miss a single bit of the scenery! Or, better still, catch the N° 83 bus at the Vieux Port. This is the successor to the old *Circulaire Corniche* tram which Dubout, the Marseilles humourist (been annexed by Montpellier just like the Rabelais whom he had illustrated) swore stopped, in his day, to allow the pétanque players to carry on with their game between the tracks! The rails and the bowls players have gone from Corniche J.F. Kennedy but the bench acknowledged as the longest in the world is still there; all two kilometres of it!

FIFTH STROLL

Musée de la marine - Quai des Belges - Quai de Rive-neuve - Bd Ch. Livon - Les Catalans - Corniche Kennedy - Monument aux Morts d'Orient - Vallon-des-Auffes - Endoume - Malmousque - Corniche Kennedy - Mémorial des Rapatriés - « Le » David - Plage du Prado - Promenade de la Plage - Bd de Bonneveine - Rond-Point - Château et parc Borély - Av. Clot-bey - Eglise Russe - Av. Alexandre Dumas - Av. de Mazargues - Av. de Haïfa - Fondation Rau - Av. de Mazargues - Av. Guy de Maupassant - Bd Michelet - Le Corbusier et la Magalonne - Rond-point du Prado - Parc Chanot - Av. du Prado - (vers centre-ville ou, facultatif) - Boulevard Périer - Bd Estrangin - Ch. du Roucas Blanc - R. du Bois-sacré - R. Pointe-à-Pitre - R. Fort-du-Sanctuaire - N.-D. de la Garde - Pl. colonel-Edon - R. Abbé Dassy - Pl. Joseph-Etienne - Av. de la Corse - R. Fort-Notre-Dame - Qu. Rive-neuve.

The Palais de la Bourse.

N.B. This quite long circuit is interrupted by two long visits ; the climb to Notre Dame de la Garde, though well-signposted, is tricky by car.

Unless wishing to end a beautiful — and long — afternoon's stroll by seeing it, I would suggest that you go some other time by the shuttle bus which goes up from Cours Jean Ballard.

Le Marseillois, Musée de la Marine.

Fishwives at the Vieux Port.

The Catalan beach in winter.

La promenade de la Corniche. →

The Château Berger on the Corniche.

I am not going to go into any more unnecessarily complicated details of your itinerary than for the previous excursion. All the same, take a map of the town with you so that you don't get lost in your car ! And keep your eyes open — there's plenty to see ! From the little beach — **La Plage des Catalans** — frequented even in winter by those hard-as-nails lovers of icy water and of handball (though the less-hardy among athletes resort to the nearby, glass-covered Cercle des Nageurs pool and facilities) along to the **Monument aux Morts d'Orient** is only a few short steps. Come and enjoy the panorama of the roadstead from under this strange triumphal arch with its soldiers by Sartorio and 'Victory' by Botinelly. In front of the islands of Frioul — Pomègues on the left and Ratonneau on the right — lies the Château d'If on its separate little isle. Much closer in and to the left are little stony islets surmounted by a curious geodesic cone. These are the Rochers des Pendus - the Rocks of the Hanged. This sinister name dates from the sacking of the town in 1423. Alphonse of Aragon had the hostages he had taken hung there before sailing away, taking with him the chain which had barred the port entrance. This can still be seen in Valencia Cathedral. The steps near the bridge lead down to the **Vallon des Auffes.** In bygone days smelly cargoes of esparto grass (auffo in Provençal) were unloaded here for use by the ropemakers. This picturesque village with its characteristic boats was created over the years by the fishermen who came from Genoa and Naples some two hundred years ago. Beloved by the composer, Vincent Scotto, who lived here, and Fernandel, who was born here, the Vallon des Auffes, with its appetising smell of bouillabaisse (the famous Marseilles fish soup) lives light-years away from the metropolis which hems it in all round about. In the summertime the rocks of the dyke are a good spot for mermaid fishing....

The military swimming pool opposite also teems with them, but the fishing is off limits there and so it is easier to try one's hand at this variety of angling over at the cove on the other side of the little **Malmousque** peninsula — that of La Fausse Monnaie !

Part of the world's longest bench.

The Vallon des Auffes from the bridge.

A pool to dream of at Malmousque.

Between the two, the mock-renaissance château in view is the headquarters of the very learned **Oceanographic Station of Endoume.** Aqua-farming research in particular is carried out here. Next, going on along the Corniche, you must from time to time tear your eyes away from the sea's enchantments and take a look at the sumptuous villas which the shipowners built themselves just over a hundred years ago. It was still 'out in the country' then and from up there one could look out for arriving sailing ships, back in those days when the wireless didn't exist. Nowadays most of these houses are occupied by organisations or, like the Villa Berger, establishments for sea water therapy. On a promontory there is the tall blade of a ship's screw. Dedicated to the French repatriates from North Africa of 1962, it was a gift to his native town from the sculptor César. This is a good spot to see the lighthouse, almost on the horizon, called Le Phare du Planier. Rebuilt since W.W.II it is possible to make out its gigantic Ionic-column shape with the aid of binoculars.

The copy of Michaelangelo's 'David' was put up with its back turned to **Prado Beach** in 1951. Quite wrongly ; though some faultfinders may think its lawns remind one more of Normandy. This area reclaimed from the polluted offshore shallows affords expansive beaches which are amongst the most beautiful on the Mediterranean and are the cleanest in France.

Further along, on the opposite side of the road is the race course — the **Hippodrome Borély.** It covers part of the park surrounding Château Borély where we are now going to stop. A lovely park with a rose garden and tall trees. Château Borély, or more correctly, **Bastide Borély,** was started in 1767 and built for a merchant of that name by the Avignon architect Esprit-Joseph Brun after the somewhat modified plans of Clérisseau. It is the biggest, most magnificent of all the country houses erected in the past out in the countrysides around Marseilles and Aix. It became an archeological museum in 1863. Its Egyptian and Greco-Roman collections have recently been moved to the Vieille Charité but its furnishings and paintings by Louis

The new Prado beaches.

Sunset ; the Prado and 'David'.

'Apostle's Head' drawing attributed to Leonardo da Vinci.

Chaix have regained their freshness and gilt. Today a museum of decorative arts and of the 18th century, it will from now on be exhibiting not only the 18th century drawings from the Feuillet de Borsat Bequest (some charming Fragonard pastels included) but also the ceramics previously kept at Musée Cantini.

From Borély we go to Avenue Mazargues (see itinerary). The Avenue de Haifa starts level with N° 508. This takes us to the **Fondation Rau** which is to open its doors in 1989. Mr Rau, doctor, philanthropist and patron of the arts, has had built an austere and functional building to house a continually expanding collection of works embracing every school from the Middle Ages up to the Impressionists and including the Italian, German, Flemish and French Renaissances.

The château Borély.

The gilded salon at the Château.

The Parc Borély racecourse.

The Rose Garden.

Boules players at the Parc Borély.

The lawns at the Parc Borély — with the chateau in the background.

Children's amusements at Prado beach.

Out in the country - the Château Pastré.

*The park at
the Château Pastré.*

Windsurfers and Sailors !

After the Fondation Rau we go by means of Avenue Maupassant to Boulevard Michelet and the nearby **Cité Radieuse** - the experimental housing block which Le Corbusier started building in 1945. Questioned at first and locally called the **Maison du Fada** or 'Crackpot's House' — this veritable self-contained town, with its shops, hotel and nursery school is nowadays much appreciated by the people who live in its 337 flats of 23 different types, and where one gets the impression of living in as many separate houses. A completely different philosophy of living is evinced on the other side of the Boulevard Michelet by the italianate villa — **'La Magalone'.** With a gigantic salon at the front it is a typical country mansion, constructed right at the end of the 17th century for the shipowning brothers Magalon — who, however, parted with it before finishing it following the plague of 1720. The ironwork, the decoration, the garden statuary and the fountains all bear the stamp of the 18th century and attest to the Italian influence.

On our return towards the centre we can pause at **Parc Chanot** if only because of the typical twenties style of its wrought iron gates. Marechal Lyautey passed through them to inaugurate the last colonial exhibition. That was before the plane-tree lined pathways led to the Palais des Congrès and the Fair of Marseille buildings — now busy with commercial activity several times a year. The nearby Stade Vélodrome is the scene of the soccer football ups and downs of the Olympique de Marseille team (Ohem !). A blue and white championship needle-match is something to be seen — if only for the atmosphere !

We can return by the **Prado** — an odd avenue designed in the 18th century and built in the 19th: its halves are at right-angles to each other. **Castellane** Fountain was sculpted by Allard (1910) and replaced the Obelisk which is now sited at Mazargues at the far end of Boulevard Michelet. This fountain demonstrates Jules Cantini's kindly though rather ostentatious patronage of the arts.

But if you risk taking **Boulevard Périer** to get

The Cantini fountain at Place Castellane.

The flower market at the Cours Pierre Puget.

76

Corlbusier's 'Cité Radieuse'.

to **Notre Dame de la Garde** you will get a good idea of the **Roucas Blanc** district - a nice place to live with its peaceful, rustic villas and gardens screened by high walls. But look out for the signs if you don't want to get lost ! In

the 17th century Notre Dame de la Garde was a fortress once governed by the brother of Melle. Scudéry. This observation post recovered its military destiny in 1944 during the Liberation when General Montsabert's

tanks and troops had to fight hard to retake the sanctuary. The showy mosaics and the thank-offering ex-voto's accumulated over 300 years, the pseudo-Byzantine basilica built by Espérandieu in 1853 may all be in questionable taste, but Notre Dame keeps its place both in the landscape and the hearts of the people of Marseilles. The gilded statue of the Virgin was added in 1870 ; it is 9m70 (31 ft) high. Its base is 12m50 (40 ft) high and

Notre-Dame de la Garde.

Ex-voto in Notre Dame de la Garde.

the tower itself is 60m (195 ft) high. If one adds the height of the rock, some 162 metres (526 ft) then the Virgin's crown is 244 metres or 792 feet above sea level !

This is **La Bonne Mère** - the good mother to whom even the veiled Muslims, who call her **'Meriêm',** come in pilgrimage. This is also and especially at sunset, the most fabulous balcony from which to look out over the entire city, the ports and the coast. Right from the cliffs of Cassis off to the east as far as Carry le Rouet and beyond to the west, since in clear weather one can see the Camargue lighthouses and even the peak of St. Loup overlooking Montpellier. Perhaps — as some swear — even the Pyrenees !

THE URGE TO TRAVEL

'Keep still so we can look each other in the eyes,
You are always ready to go though
Held by these anchors
Which tie you to the shore and nibble you beneath the sea !

Thus wrote Jules Supervielle in 1928. Did it take a poet to understand that Marseilles can only be explained by the sea ? Turned towards the sea and fascinating, but in some ways fragile, because of it ? Marseilles is the leading French port. It dealt with 91 million tonnes in 1987 compared with the 53 million tonnes of Le Havre and the 32 million tonnes of Dunkerque. It is the sixth in the world ; though it has 2 1/2 times less traffic than Rotterdam, its traffic is still with in the order of value of those of Yokohama and Nagoya — being but roughly ten per cent short of them. Even if the hydrocarbons passing through Fos-sur-Mer must be taken into account, this is reassuring. Nevertheless, the succession of big docks which we are going to see to the north-west of the Greco-Latin town give a singular im-pression if not of being abandoned, at least of being uninhabited. To correct this idea, and without denying the worldwide slump and profound crisis in ship repair and construction, one must bear in mind the irreversible technical developments which have taken place. All these quays were built in the not-so-far off times when passenger transport to Africa and the East was solely by sea. Today the survival of the ferries to Corsica and Algiers and Tunis is due to the transport of cars and trucks. Everything else goes by 'plane from Marseille — Provence International Airport at Marignane. As to goods cargoes — most of these don't enter a warehouse. Goods are transported either loaded already onto trucks (roll-on, roll-off) or in containers which are im-mediately transferred to elsewhere by the railway.

SIXTH STROLL

La Bourse (P) - Cours Belsunce - Rue d'Aix - Pl. Jules-Guesdes - Les Grands Carmes (à pied) - Bd des Dames - Bd de la Major - Bd de Dunkerque - Autoroute du Littoral - Chemin du Littoral - L'Estaque - Le Rove retour par le même itinéraire jusqu'au tunnel qu'on évite pour revenir au point de départ par le Quai du Port.

Returning by the same route until the tunnel, which we miss out, we go back to our starting point via the Quai du Port. It is only on our right, as we leave the Centre Bourse, that Cours Belsunce has preserved the frontages — now looking far from at their best — of the fine carriage-way which was once able — in the 17th century — to rival that of Aix. It is hard to recognise the façade of the once-famous 'Alcazar' music hall where Maurice Chevalier, Fernandel, Yves Montand and so many others once appeared. At the point where the roadway narrows and becomes the Rue d'Aix there is a façade and supporting caryatids carved in the Pugets' workshops.

Porte d'Aix — the Arc de Triomphe.

L'église des Grandes Carmes.

The famous Marseilles soap.

The Joliette Quay and the 19th century docks.

The beaconlight at the end of the jetty.

The commercial port basins.

Ships ready to sail.

On the dock.

Rue d'Aix emerges at the Place Jules Guesde roundabout. The triumphal Arch of 1825, with carvings by David d'Angers, replaces the original **Porte d'Aix** — a gateway in the 17th century town wall. At the end of the northern motorway, on a wall across from the Arch, there is a mural construction carried out by the Groupe Artifice in 1983. This shows the first of two galleys, each constructed in 24 hours — a record time. The first galley was made in 1677 before the minister of the Navy, Mr Seignelay. The

second — but was it really a galley — on the occasion of the visit of the Austrian emperor Joseph II in 1777. In the courtyard of the Hôtel de Région there are the 17th century arches, in rib form, of the aqueduct over the Huveaune, and three courses of the Greek ramparts. At the near-at-hand Church des Grands Carmes (1620), built on an ancient temple's foundations, the notable features are the portal by Pierre Poisson, 1648, the altar and baroque woodwork by the Duparcs, respectively of the 18th and 17th centuries,

The interchange at the Gare Maritime.

and the pictures by Michel Serre (Life of the Virgin; end of 17th century). The organ, dating from the same period, awaits restoration.

Let's go back to the car; **Boulevard des Dames** — with its unpredictable traffic — preserves memories of the Bastion des Dames — the Women's Barricade — built by women during the siege of the town by Charles Quint in 1536. The boulevard intersects Rue de la République. Bearing right and turning onto Boulevard de Dunkerque, we take the ramp onto the autoroute du Littoral. We stay on this until l'Estaque. This was exclusively a fishing port until recently. Georges Braque the artist frequented the port at the start of the cubist period in 1908. Cezanne also painted here — notably a canvas now belonging to the Fondation Rau (cf above). Passing by the premises of Comex, world leaders in underwater work at great depths, and after l'Estaque we tackle the bends of the cliff road until we reach the road tunnel through the cliffs of the Rove. From this point we can take in at a glance the entire line of docks of the Port of Marseilles. Here they are, going from the nearest to the farthest : l'Estaque, the dry docks for cleaning and repair at the northern outer port, with the Saumaty inlet — the new fishing port and fish market behind. Next comes Mirabeau dock, level with the deepwater jetty, counterpart of Quay Léon Gouret. Then follow President Wilson Dock, Pinède Dock and the one-time Imperial Dock now Le Bassin National. These are each divided in two by a quay. Further back are the dry docks, then the dock for the Gare Maritime d'Arenc and finally the long dock of La Grande Joliette, overlooked by the Cathedral and reaching right to the foot of Fort St. Jean.

As we return to the centre, along the motorway, we will be able to look down upon the docks and see in greater detail the subjects of our trip.

The Rove tunnel.

Jousting at L'Estaque harbour.

The fishing port of Les Goudes.

MARSEILLES — OUT AND ABOUT

Marseilles is very big... On maps one notices
with surprise that this tentacular city doesn't
only take in lines of streets, factories and
quays, but also villages, fields, hills that look
like steep mountains, desert lands and woods.
It is not all that long ago that, in the morning
and less than a kilometre from the church of
Les Réformés, one's car's tyres skidded on
dung left by a flock of sheep. The village so
dear to Marcel Pagnol — La Treille — hasn't
changed since the time of 'Papet' and 'Manon
des Sources'. As to the Goudes, to
Callelongue and the calanques (a series of
deep set rocky inlets that follow), a Greek
friend of mine who lives in Rue Paradis puts
his hiking boots on every Sunday and goes off
to rediscover the air and the light of the
Peloponnese there. You'll have no problem
finding the way to La Treille yourself, going
by the Station Thermale des Camoins to
which Bonaparte and Désirée Clary both
went, and where, later, Charles IV King of
Spain used to come during his exile in a
carriage drawn by mules.
But, since one must make a choice, to find an
unknown aspect of Marseilles, we may as well

Callelongue.

Sormiou.

Morgiou.

Sugiton.

follow the seashore. Our previous excursion, the last of those in which we explored together the urban fabric of Marseilles, followed the Promenade de la Plage along the beach until we reached the crossroads at Bonneveine. There it turned off. This time we will continue to follow the sea shore along the *Avenue de Montredon.* After about 1.2 kilometres from the Bonneveine round-about a turning on the right, at the traffic light, leads you to the Pointe Rouge Port de Plaisance (Avenue Odessa). Here you can see some beautiful yachts and watch windsurfing champions practising. Perhaps you can come another day and stay longer. Now I suggest we continue along Avenue de Montredon. A little farther along on the left, an open gateway invites you to enter a tree-lined avenue. This is the *Campagne Pastré.* This immense park is now municipal property and covers part of the mountainous hill-range of Marseilleveyre. There are two turn-of-the-century châteaux, a huge country house where the town receives its important guests, and a riding centre. This spot is laden with history. During the last war refugee musicians and artists were sheltered here by Countess Pastré — descendant of an old shipowning family. A form of patronage all the more praiseworthy since she risked her life in so doing ! This typifies a certain kind of Marseillaise elegance. Unfortunately there isn't time to linger beneath the trees or on the banks of the canal. We must go on. From here the road becomes the Avenue de la Madrague de Montredon. In days gone by a 'madrague' (from the arab word 'almazraba' for enclosure) consisted of a maze of nets set up on the shore and in which tuna fish became trapped. Inside, in the last enclosure a huge, horizontal, square net could be lifted using a wooden device. In use all along the Mediterranean coast, this kind of fishing was done collectively according to a cooperative agreement, but was originally subject of a lord's rights. It was in this way that the hamlet which Boulevard de la Grotte Roland traverses came into being ; around a madrague. From this point the Chemin de la Baume (which means the same as Grotto) Roland begins, and is the starting point for

Cliff climbing.

some quite dangerous expeditions. But the actual Port de la Madrague is to be found farther along. Farther still is the fishing village, **Les Goudes,** with its narrow streets, at right angles, its tiny houses and little port of which the pot-bellied boats are identical to those in the Bay of Naples, and to those in the Vallon des Auffes, with the same phallic motif carved on the prow. From here the coast road becomes narrow and winding until it reaches **Callelongue.**

This is another fishing hamlet — smaller and wilder than the previous one. It is dominated by a beacon perched on a natural pyramid. A path winds round the foot of this hill. This trail is quite safe though it isn't advised for those without a good head for heights and good foot wear. It leads via the Calanque du Podestat to that of Cortiou. To reach the calanque of Sormiou, on the other hand, one takes Avenue de Mazargues from opposite

The calanque at En-Vau.

the intersection of Rue Paradis with Le Prado, and continues along Le Chemin du Roi d'Espagne and the Chemin de Sormiou. Just before the famous prison of Les Baumettes with its feartul reputation, taking the road to the right leads one to the calanque of Morgiou. However, to reach the calanque of Sugiton the easiest access is by way of the Route de Cassis (Avenue Maréchal de Lattre de Tassigny) the extension of Boulevard Michelet after the Mazargues obelisk. On the right the Chemin de Luminy goes on up to the fine buildings of the university campus of that name. As to three other of the calanques — Port Miou, Port Pin and En Vau, access to these is either by the foresters' track from the Col de la Gardiole reached via the Col de la Gineste on the old road to Cassis — the D559, or by way of Cassis itself. Whichever way one goes, the final stage can only be on foot !

The calanques — deep indentations in a savage coastline — are sparsely inhabited. The few cabins are surrounded by steep cliffs, the silence broken by the clinking of rock climbers' gear. The water is limpid — incredibly so at Sugiton and En Vau, backs-of-beyond where nudists believe they are living once more in an earthly paradise.

In the sea's salty water here are mysterious resurgences — perhaps linked to the underground systems of the Fontaine de Vaucluse... Arthur Rimbaud remembered this when he wrote : ***'The river at Cassis rolls, unsuspected, in strange vales !...*** he wrote this in 1872, yet he was not to come to Marseilles until 1891, to die there.

95

Allauch village.

An old mill at Allauch.

The 13 Christmas-tide desserts.

L'adieu to the crèche at Château Gombert.

La Pastorale — a Provençal tradition.

A Provençal crèche.

BY CAR

Villages still exist around Marseilles. Château Gombert can be reached by way of Longchamp, Les Chutes Lavie and Saint Jérôme. A mecca of folklore, where each year on the fête of St. Eloi - the 2nd Sunday in June - a richly decorated harness, called the **gaillardet** is auctioned off keenly. There is a museum of folklore where you will learn at least one thing - the correct list of the 13 traditional desserts to follow Christmas

St. Jean's Fire at Allauch.

Dinner as the custom is in Provence ! The 17th century church at Château Gombert is well-endowed with paintings by Michel Serre, Finsonius and the sculptor Pierre Puget's son, François. The narrow roads beyond lead into the Étoile range of mountains. Don't miss the underground caverns of Les Grottes Loubières - the mysterious setting of Raymond Jean's novel *'La Fontaine Obscure'*. Next, Allauch, another village for Christmas crib 'santon' figurines. To get there take the eastern autoroute — the one for Toulon.

Come off at La Valentine and follow the road for Les Camoins. At Allauch itself there is a 12th century church, another of the 17th century as well as wind-mills, a museum in an 18th century house and perhaps best of all, a pedestrian itinerary in the hills behind linking all the spots made famous by Marcel Pagnol: La Baume Sourne, Le Garlaban and from Aubagne to La Treille all the sites (from *'Château de ma mère'* to *'La Gloire de mon Père'*) which punctuated the childhood and work of the author of 'Manon des Sources'.

99

Embarking for the Isles.

The Château d'If seen from Notre Dame de la Garde.

Malmousque and the Frioul archipelago.

The ruins of the Hopital Caroline — a onetime lazaret — on the isle of Ratonneau.

THE ISLANDS

Ratonneau, Pomègues, the Château d'If (together forming the Frioul archipelago), the Rochers des Pendus off the Vallon des Auffes, the islet of Tiboulen (look hard — is hidden behind Pomègues), the islet Degaby (just a word here — is not true that the cross on top of the little fort surmounts the tomb of the singer, Gaby Deslys) ; the Ile Maire, rocky home for wild goats, separated from Les Goudes at Cap Croisette by a narrow strait ; and near at hand, like a chick and its mother-hen, another Tiboulen — not to be mixed up with the first ! Some way over to the south-east are the marine counter parts of the Marseilleveyre Range — the islands of Jarron, Jarre, Calseraigne and Riou, the latter surrounded with reefs upon which more than one ancient vessel foundered — creating an archeological divers' delight. Then Moyade, Les Empereurs, little and big Congloué where roam the ghosts of Markos Sestios, the Greek navigator, and the captain of the 'Grand St. Antoine' whose ship brought the Plague in 1720 ! The best-hidden islet, however, is the ***Torpilleur,*** anchored in the Calanque of Sugiton....

The Islands of Marseilles — mini-cruises. For the price of a bus ticket you can have the world's cheapest cruise on the ferry between the Town Hall and Place aux Huiles. Five minutes to dream of the Leeward Islands, of Marius and Captain Escartefigue, the famous characters of Marcel Pagnol. Joking aside, though it is dearer it is still reasonably cheap to board one of the white motor launches which run more or less regularly to Château d'If and Port Frioul. At the Château d'If, built by François I, one hour is sufficient for musing in front of the imaginary cells of The Count of Monte Cristo and the Abbot, Faria, as well as before the real ones of the prisoners of the 1848 revolution and the Commune. Over the Château float memories of several famous 'guests'. After Iron Mask famed if nameless prisoner of the time of King Louis XIV, Mirabeau was imprisoned here. The rhinocerous given by the King of Portugal to Pope Léon X, and which Albrecht

Arriving at Château d'If.

Maïre island.

102

Island greenery.

The Frioul islands and the dyke.

103

Durer later drew, was penned up here. In 1800 the remains of Kléber rested here for some time after his assassination by a fanatic in Egypt. A few cable-lengths away, the Frioul dyke joining the two islands into one, with its 360 metres of quay makes a harbour bigger than the Old Port. At one time a military base, Pomègues is crossed by a road 3 kilometres long (closed to motor vehicles).

century this was enlarged into being a joint hospital-hotel-prison camp — *l'Hôpital Caroline,* built around its Greek temple-styled chapel. Les Compagnons du Devoir are carefully restoring this romantic ruin, with its double-turn ramp linking it to the cemetery for plague victims. Beautiful beaches lie beyond.

But what about the other islands ? You'll

Islands in the mist.

This links a fort to a beacon. There are some good beaches suitable for bathing to the north except, however, when the Mistral wind is blowing.

On Ratonneau Island there is a discrete village of holiday homes close to the quay between some sports facilities and the harbour pilots' hotel. In Roman times this was an outer port (Forum Julii). Later a Lazareth was established and in the 19th

need Marseillais friends to take you to them by yacht or motor boat. In summertime you'll also find motor launches which 'do the calanques'. Obviously the most amusing way would be to go with a fisherman from Les Goudes or Callelongue. It depends on how much time you've got. In any case it is something not to be missed — and to end up knowing Marseilles better than most of the people who live there do !

Farewell to the islands.

PICTURE CREDITS

Alfred WOLF

p.p. 13 (haut), 15 (bas), 17 (haut), 18/19, 24 (haut), 27 (haut), 30 (bas g.), 31, 37 (bas), 38 (bas), 40, 44/45, 52 (haut), 57 (haut), 60 (bas d.), 66 (bas), 67 (haut), 72 (bas g.), 81, 82/83, 84 (haut g.), 84 (bas), 86, 88/89, 92/93 (bas), 103 (bas g.).

**Photosynthèse
Christian CRÈS**

p.p. couverture, 6/7, 10/11, 13 (bas), 15, 21 (haut), 22, 23, 25 (haut), 28, 30 (haut g.), 32, 33, 35 (haut), 36, 48 (haut), 49 (bas), 50 (haut), 51 (haut), 52 (bas), 55 (haut), 56, 57 (bas), 59 (haut), 61, 62, 63, 67 (bas), 68/69, 70 (haut), 71 (haut), 74 (haut), 76 (haut), 79 (haut), 92/93 (haut), 94/95, 96, 97 (haut), 98 (gauche), 100 (bas), 101 (bas), 102/103 (haut).

Pierre CIOT

p.p. 8/9, 20, 54, 73 (haut), 74 (bas), 75 (bas g.), 77, 84/85 (haut), 90/91, 104.

**IMASUD
Laurent GIRAUDOU**

p.p. 14 (haut), 16 (bas), 29 (bas), 30 (bas), 34, 36/37, 38 (haut), 39, 42, 43, 47, 48 (bas), 49 (haut), 50 (bas), 51 (droite), 55 (bas), 59 (bas), 60 (haut), 72 (bas d.), 73 (bas), 75 (haut), 75 (bas d.), 76 (bas), 82 (gauche), 85 (bas), 97 (bas), 98 (haut), 98/99, 101 (haut), 103 (bas d.).

Thierry IBERT

p.p. 64 (haut), 78, 79 (bas), 88 (gauche), 91 (droite), 100 (haut).

J.-M. ANTOINE

p.p. 30 (haut), 64 (bas), 102 (bas).

Collection des Musées de Marseille

p.p. 17 (bas) photo Yves GALLOIS, 21 (bas), 25 (bas) Yves GALLOIS, 35 (bas), 46 (haut) Serge SARACCO, 46 (bas), 51 (bas), 58 (haut), 58 (bas) Yves GALLOIS, 60 (bas g.), 63 (droite), 70 (bas), 71 (bas).

L. SCIARLI, photos aériennes

p.p. 4/5, 41, 65, 105.

Serge BORRELLY

p.p. 16, 25 (bas), 26, 27 (bas), 29 (haut), 53, 66 (haut), 72 (haut), 87.

Achevé d'imprimé le 10 juin 1988
sur les presses d'Intergraphie
à Saint-Etienne

Photogravure : Société Provençale de Photogravure

Photocomposition : aztec

Maquette : Apache

Photo de couverture : Photosynthèse C. Crès

Dépôt légal : 2e trimestre 1988